U2
4 THE PEOPLE

by Tony Scott

CHERRY LANE Books INC

Cherry Lane Books, Port Chester, NY 10573
First Printing 1985
Printed in the United States of America

Editorial Direction by TONY SCOTT
Art Direction and design by AMID CAPECI
Production Coordination by Joan McCann

Published by: Cherry Lane Books
               110 Midland Avenue
               Port Chester, NY 10573

INTRODUCTION

On July 13, 1985, as the midday sun shone brightly over the John F. Kennedy Stadium in Philadelphia, the 90,000-strong crowd that had gathered to witness the North American Live Aid concert cheered loudly when Hollywood actor Jack Nicholson appeared onstage. Casually attired in a black shirt, black pants and black shades, the movie star addressed the audience, which had just witnessed an excellent performance by Canadian rocker Bryan Adams. Nicholson was not only seen by the Philadelphia crowd, but also by countless television viewers around the world and by the thousands of fans who were at London's Wembley Stadium watching the British Live Aid show.

After acknowledging Bryan Adams, Jack Nicholson announced: "And now, to keep with the international and global feeling that we have, a group direct from London. A group whose heart is in Dublin, Ireland, and whose spirit is with the world. A group that's never had any problem saying how they feel . . . U2!"

Those watching the Live Aid musical extravaganza on MTV in the United States then heard the voice of VJ Mark Goodman, who stated: "This has to be the first transatlantic MC by Jack Nicholson. And everybody around the world is looking forward to this band especially—U2, now taking the stage at Wembley in London, as Live Aid continues."

Meanwhile, onstage at Wembley, the members of U2 were busy tuning their instruments. After Larry Mullen had finished banging his drums, the Edge had strummed a few chords on his guitar and Adam Clayton was through pounding his bass, a famous British DJ declared: "From the Live Aid stage, London, here is a band from the Republic of Ireland with international respect and appeal. Ladies and gentlemen . . . U2!"

There was an incredible feeling of excitement around the globe as lead singer Bono, who was dressed in a black military jacket and leather strides, strolled up to the microphone and introduced the song *Sunday Bloody Sunday*. As the Edge unleashed the tune's haunting guitar riff over Larry Mullen's military-style drumbeat, the Wembley crowd literally erupted. "How long? How long must we sing this song?" sang Bono, and, although the words had originally been written about the tragic days in Ireland's history, they could so easily be applied to the plight of the Ethiopian famine victims.

Midway through *Sunday Bloody Sunday*, Bono grabbed a cameraman from the side of the stage and brought him forward, encouraging him to point his lens toward the audience. The singer then jumped out onto the lower section of the stage and rallied the crowd to sing the words to the song. After returning to his microphone stand when the tune was finished, Bono announced: "We're an Irish band, we come from Dublin city, Ireland. Like all cities, it has its good and it has its bad. This song is called *Bad*."

The number's moody atmospherics were perfect for the Live Aid concert and there could be no doubt that U2 was turning in a truly memorable performance. Once again, Bono could not restrain himself from trying to get closer to the fans and, halfway through *Bad*, he actually jumped into the photographer's pit. At one point, he seemed to be taking charge of the security guards, as he motioned for them to help some of the front row fans who were being crushed. Before long, he was actually dancing with a couple of young girls from the audience.

The charismatic frontman then began singing the lyrics to Lou Reed's *Walk On The Wild Side* and the Stones' *Ruby Tuesday*. Finally, as U2's 20-minute set neared its completion, Bono made his exit and said, "God bless you all!" as he left the stage waving a towel.

Bono and U2 had risen to the occasion and, ultimately, the band's performance proved to be one of the best of the day. However, it is hardly surprising that the Irish rockers triumphed, since they have spent the past five years proving to music fans around the globe that U2 is very much a people's band. There is a sincerity to the group's music that is unlike that of any other act in the business.

Originally hailing from Dublin, the four musicians didn't form a band because they envisioned that they would sell millions of albums and attain superstar notoriety. Sure, deep down inside, they may have dreamed about "hitting the big time," but, essentially, they got together to play music and to escape the ennui of everyday life. As the Edge has so often stated, "We had no idea it would become a profession."

In many respects, U2 has become a profession for the Edge, Bono, Adam and Larry. After all, it pays their living costs and prevents them from having to take "normal" jobs. But the U2 members are more concerned with artistic creativity, rather than the pursuit of money. As Bono told *Rolling Stone* magazine in a 1985 interview: "I don't have a million dollars in my pocket or in my bank account. I don't want to say that money is not important to me, because it is disgusting for me to say that at a time when a lot of people don't have money. So I'm thankful that I don't have to worry about my next meal. It *is* a threat to the band, because I don't want anything to take away from our focus."

U2 has never feared writing about the world's problems, but the band knows that a four or five-minute song probably won't have a drastic effect upon the world in which we live. "Honestly, the whole U2 phenomenon is probably going to amount to little real change," the Edge told Britain's *N.M.E.* "I think we're quite sanguine about that, but that's not the only reason we would be doing this. We're doing it because it's worth doing and we think it's the right thing to do."

This book tells the U2 story, from the early days in Dublin to the group's current high-ranking status in the world of contemporary music.

U2 . . . 4 the people!

CHAPTER I

The history of U2 dates back to 1976, when a pupil at Dublin's Mount Temple Comprehensive School, named Larry Mullen Jr., posted a sign on one of the notice boards declaring his intention of forming a rock band. Although he was only 15 at the time, the young lad had been hooked on music from an early age and had taken an active interest in playing the drums.

Shortly after he had begun his quest for other aspiring musicians, Larry was approached by three fellow Mount Temple students—Paul "Bono Vox" Hewson, David "The Edge" Evans and Adam Clayton. Despite the fact that the drummer was a couple of years younger than his musical comrades, he felt no sense of intimidation since none of them could play particularly well at the time.

Bono later told a reporter an amusing anecdote about one of the band's early rehearsal sessions, which took place in the drummer's kitchen. Apparently, a group of teenage girls kept looking through the window at Larry, who eventually became so annoyed that he dismissed them with a garden hose! Evidently, at this juncture, playing the drums was far more important to him than courting females.

Following a brief series of rehearsals, the band made its very first appearance at a school talent contest. Calling themselves Feedback, the four members played a version of Peter Frampton's *Show Me The Way*, which elicited extremely positive response from the audience. Although their playing abilities may have been limited, the excitement was sufficient to make the lads want to master their instruments and take their music seriously. Bono has since referred to the gig as "a very special concert." There was definitely a spark and according to the singer: "We built ourselves around that spark."

Bono, the second son of a Protestant mother and a Catholic father, was raised in Ballymun, a working-class district located within the city limits of Dublin. He was nicknamed "Bono Vox" (which he later shortened to simply "Bono") by a local gangmember called Guggi, whose younger brother actually appeared on the front cover photographs of U2's BOY and WAR albums. Bono claims that, to this day, he is still uncertain what "Bono Vox" referred to, although one imagines that it may well have had something to do with his mouth. The singer has never denied that he has always been a good deal more talkative than the average person!

At the age of 15, Bono's life was turned upside down by the death of his mother. He has told the press that after she died things were never quite the same in the Hewson household. He has further stated that, from that point, he no longer viewed his house as a home. It was simply a *house*.

While his father endeavored to keep the family together, Bono found himself getting into numerous fights with his brother, some of which were positively violent. His attitude to the outside world began to change dramatically. Like the other future U2 members, Bono was convinced that there had to be a means of escaping from the dull, dreary and depressing environment in which they were growing up.

As he explained to one reporter from *Rolling Stone* magazine: "We grew up on a street where people got a job, got married, had children ... and died. And went to the pub. We'd meet a guy, he'd say, 'Drinking? Oh yeah, drinking Thursday night, drinking Friday night, drinking Saturday night, drinking Sunday morning after Mass, drinking Sunday night. Back to the jar on Tuesday night.' We would see this. And we just said, 'We will not become a part of this.' "

Bono has also been quoted as saying that U2 was always "anti-laziness" and "anti-apathy with no direction."

During the band's early days, Bono had reportedly been keen to play lead guitar, but it wasn't long before that role had been assumed by Dave Evans. Generally known as "The Edge" ("It's basically part of my teenage heritage," he says. "It was one of those nicknames that just stuck—I think it was Bono who gave it to me."), Dave's musical career began on the piano when he was 11. He subsequently took lessons, but by the time he reached his teens he had given up tickling the ivories.

It was only a matter of time before he turned his attention towards the guitar. Initially inspired by listening to Rory Gallagher records, which he borrowed from a friend, the Edge's musical taste gradually broadened. Nowadays, he cites Robert Fripp, Adrian Belew and Holger Czukay as his favorite players. He is also particularly keen on Tom Verlaine's work during Television's MARQUEE MOON period.

Although the Edge's father was (and still is) a member of the Dublin Welsh Male Voice Choir, he has said that he didn't really come from a strong musical background. However, by the time he was strumming a guitar, his older brother, Dik, had also picked up the instrument. In fact, since money was so hard to come by, the two brothers were forced to share the same guitar and amplifier.

While the Edge, Bono and Larry had basically grown up in a working-class environment, Adam Clayton came from a rather more affluent background and grew up in the district of Malahide. His parents had ensured that he was educated privately and, after attending a preparatory school, he became a boarder at St. Columba's School. He has since claimed that he rebelled

against the "privileged society"at St. Columba's and that he found the teachers and their strong religious indoctrination somewhat hard to handle. Eventually, Adam ended up leaving when he was 16 and he became a student at Mount Temple in Dublin.

When Adam connected with Larry Mullen Jr.'s new band, he immediately had an edge over the other members since he was the only one who had previously played in a group. According to Bono though, the bassist relied a good deal on the "art of bluff." Apparently, he would use words like "gig" and talk about things like his "action," which immediately convinced the others that he was a skilled player. As it turned out, his musical abilities weren't really much better than anyone else's and he had allegedly been fired from his first group, the Max Quad Band, because he couldn't play. It seems, however, that Adam basically couldn't conform to playing conventional rhythms and it was this factor that ultimately led him to develop an extremely unique style of his own.

As soon as Adam, Larry, Bono and the Edge started practicing together, so their musical talents began to grow. The Edge has always assessed that the band was terrible

in its early days, but the limits of their technical capabilities helped them to develop their own individual styles within the context of the group. Because they had all started out at the same time, they had yet to establish their own identities and, consequently, there was no problem of clashing egos.

It was through playing music together that the four lads became friends. Drawing from various influences, they essentially made the most of what they had and as Bono told Irish journalist Liam Mackey: "We were four completely different people, four people going nowhere and we decided to go there together ... the only thing we had in common was the music."

Making music became so addictive that they gradually placed less and less importance on their academic studies. Although their parents, particularly Adam Clayton's, may have been concerned, the teaching staff at Mount Temple turned out to be extremely supportive of the band's musical endeavors. Since it was Dublin's first comprehensive (government-subsidized) school, and was both coeducational and nondenominational, Mount Temple was a rather unconventional establishment, which clearly worked in the group's favor.

After making their debut public appearance at the school talent contest, the four young musicians continued to rehearse and, if they were lucky, they would get to play the occasional gig in church halls. Somewhere along the line, they changed their name to the Hype.

During these early days, club work for bands that played original material was almost non-existent on the Irish rock scene. The major influences and trends tended to come from London. Most of the new Irish acts were "garage bands" who basically played for the fun of it all, knowing full well that if they really wanted to make it then they would have to travel abroad, either to Britain or America.

Towards the end of 1976, the British music industry found itself in the midst of the new wave/punk rock explosion. Bono has since claimed that he had actually felt a change coming within the music business and he was delighted when Johnny Rotten and the Sex Pistols burst onto the scene with *Anarchy In the U.K.,* which was essentially the first "punk anthem."

Bono has openly admitted that he had an extrovert personality and he was reportedly the first punk rocker at Mount Temple. One day, he allegedly turned up wearing

PAiSTe

bright colored pants and a 60s jacket, with his hair cropped short and a chain hanging from one of his ears to his nose! Quite simply, he viewed the punk rock movement as an excellent vehicle for individual expression.

In the wake of the British punk rock revolution, several bands had made their way across the Irish channel to London. First came the Undertones and Stiff Little Fingers, both of whom hailed from Belfast. Then followed the emergence of Dublin's the Radiators From Space, who scored a deal with London's highly respected independent label, Chiswick Records. However, it was Bob Geldof's Boomtown Rats who put Dublin back on the rock'n'roll map in September 1977 with the Top 20 British chart smash *Looking Out For Number One*. Geldof, who has of course since achieved notoriety as the mastermind behind the Band Aid and Live Aid projects, quickly became a star and the Rats enjoyed a string of hits, including the number one single, *I Don't Like Mondays*.

Life may have been a good deal easier for Bono, the Edge, Larry Mullen Jr. and Adam Clayton had they been based in London, since Dublin wasn't particularly receptive towards new bands. Nevertheless, as time went by, they managed to get gigs on a more frequent basis. More often than not, the Hype would have to play two sets, one consisting of cover tunes and the other comprising original material. Their cover set included songs like *Jumpin' Jack Flash, Suffragette City, Anarchy In The U.K., Heart Of Gold* and *2-4-6-8 Motorway*. However, the Edge has said that they were one of the world's worst cover bands. In fact, he told one reporter that they began writing more and more of their own numbers, simply because they were so bad at playing other people's material.

After a while, the Hype became known as U2, apparently at the suggestion of Steve Rapids from the Radiators From Space. Bono has revealed that the name was chosen because of its ambiguous qualities and also because it couldn't be linked to any particular trend. The band could quite easily have passed itself off as a "new wave" act, but Bono declared: "We want to stand up on our own."

CHAPTER II

During the early months of 1978, U2 continued to play local gigs wherever and whenever possible. Although the band had yet to establish itself as the "Next Big Thing" to come out of Dublin, the tide was beginning to turn.

In March, the group entered the *Evening Press/Harp Lager* talent contest, which was held on St. Patrick's Day and was part of the Limerick Civic Week festivities. The winning act would not only receive 500 pounds, but it would also have the opportunity to record a demo tape and audition for the Irish division of CBS Records.

Around 40 bands participated, with the initial heats held during the day. In the evening, the finalists performed a few of their songs in front of a panel of judges, which included the CBS representative, Jackie Hayden. U2 came through the early rounds with flying colors and then competed for the top prize with bands like Room Service and the East Coast Angels. While their competitors may have been better musicians, U2 came across with a tremendous amount of energy, which impressed the judges (particularly Hayden) and landed them in first place.

Several weeks after the *Evening Press/Harp Lager* contest, U2 spent a day at Dublin's Keystone Studios. The basic idea was to record about 10 numbers "live" so that CBS could judge the band's potential. It was their first experience in a recording studio and it appears that the band members weren't particularly enthralled by the event. The Edge apparently suffered tuning problems throughout the session, which was eventually brought to an abrupt end when Larry Mullen's father came to pick up his son because he had to go to school the following day. Time had been limited in the studio and the end result precipitated a complete lack of interest from CBS Ireland.

Despite the fact that CBS turned the band down, Bono and Adam Clayton are said to have called up Jackie Hayden a few weeks later. From the outset, Hayden had been able to recognize U2's immense potential and, consequently, he decided to send them a standard CBS contract. However, Adam then met the record executive in his office and said that the band wasn't keen to sign the contract. Because they were young, they wanted to wait before committing themselves. While most bands would have jumped at the opportunity to score a record deal, U2 was clearly a group that was prepared to wait until it felt the time was right, which was probably an extremely prudent course of action.

Although the band had opted not to sign with CBS, there was to be no such hesitation in hooking up with a manager. Irish journalist Bill Graham, who was one of the first music business people to take an active interest in U2, introduced the band to Paul McGuinness, whose previous track record included working with the folk rock group Spud, as well as with an American singer/songwriter named Thom Moore. McGuinness had also directed a number of advertising films, but when he met up with the members of U2 he was eager to handle their affairs.

However, despite the acquisition of a manager, U2 still found it very tough to get a break during the latter part of 1978. After their victory at the *Evening Press/Harp Lager* competition, the four musicians managed to secure a series of opening dates with the Stranglers and the Greedy Bastards (a pick-up band featuring Thin Lizzy's Philip Lynott). For the major part though, they found themselves being restricted by the distinct lack of energy and excitement on the Dublin scene.

In December '78, the group paid its second visit to a recording studio. All of the members had left school by this stage, so Larry didn't have to worry about his dad coming over to collect him! Barry Devlin, a member of the Irish band Horslips, was hired to produce a new demo tape, which featured three original compositions—*Street Missions, Shadows In Tall Trees* and *The Fool*. The session went extremely well and it wasn't long before people were predicting that U2 was on the verge of landing a major record deal.

Jackie Hayden at CBS, together with Paul McGuinness, managed to persuade the record company's UK division to send an A&R representative named Nicky Graham over to Dublin to check out the band. Graham was impressed, and it wasn't long before CBS U.K. agreed to have Chas De Whalley, who had previously been a writer for the British weekly music magazine *Sounds*, fly over and produce some more demos at Dublin's Windmill Lane

Studios. Under De Whalley's guidance, U2 recorded another three original songs—*Boy Girl*, *Stories For Boys* and *Out Of Control*.

Despite the initial interest, CBS U.K. decided not to sign the band, at which point Jackie Hayden suggested that the Chas De Whalley-produced demos be packaged as a 12-inch record for the Irish market. There were minimal costs involved, since the demo tapes had already been paid for by CBS in Britain.

Aside from the 12-inch version, which was to be released in a limited edition of 1,000 numbered copies, a seven-inch version was also prepared. U2's debut Ep, *U2:3*, finally reached record stores in September 1979 and, within a few days of its release, it had become Ireland's biggest selling 12-inch single ever. Sales of the seven-inch were also strong and *U2:3* eventually topped the Irish charts.

The band was featured on the front cover of *Hot Press*, Ireland's leading rock music publication, and editor Niall Stokes enthused: "Such has been the consistency of their development that they now stand on the brink of an international breakthrough, at an average age of less than nineteen."

Despite such praise in their native country, CBS U.K. still failed to show any interest in them. Paul McGuinness had, however, organized a series of British dates towards the end of 1979, which were due to be financed by a publishing advance. Unfortunately, problems arose when the money from the publishing company was cut drastically, forcing the manager to borrow a considerable amount of cash from family and friends in order to send the band to Britain. U2 finally arrived in London at the end of November and played a brief series of club gigs. At this juncture, there were those who believed that the band might have been wise to set up base in the British capital, but the individual members found that they weren't particularly comfortable with the idea of living there and that they felt somewhat alienated.

As 1979 turned into 1980, the buzz on the streets was that it could only be a matter of time before U2 landed a major international recording contract. However, during the early weeks of the new year, potential deals with EMI and A&M Records failed to materialize, leaving the band feeling more than a little demoralized. The group's cashflow had deteriorated but, refusing to wallow in self-pity, there was to be no turning back at this stage.

A second CBS Ireland single, *Another Day* (b/w *Twilight*), was released and in February, 1980, U2 decided to take the bold step of embarking on a headline tour of its native country. Bono claimed that he and the rest of the band wanted to show people that they had definitely not lost their confidence.

When U2 headlined the Dublin Stadium in March, an executive from Island Records was in the audience and, according to Bono, he offered the group a deal immediately after the show.

The Island Records company had been founded back in the 1960s by Chris Blackwell, who wanted to introduce Jamaican ska/reggae music to Britain. Towards the end of the decade, he became involved with rock groups and subsequently signed acts like Traffic, King Crimson, Free, Fairport Convention, Mott The Hoople and Roxy Music (featuring Bryan Ferry). During the late 70s, Island released albums by Ultravox and Eddie & The Hot Rods and, by the time U2 was approached by the label, its roster included Marianne Faithful, Robert Palmer, Grace Jones and the B-52's.

Believe it or not, U2 allegedly complained about the terms of the contract that was offered by the company! However, Island Records was prepared to negotiate and it wasn't long before the band had been signed. The press reported that it was a four year/four album deal, at the end of which the label could decide whether or not it wanted to keep the group. The 1980 game plan was for U2 to release a number of singles and record an album in August, which would hit the streets in October.

As the Edge told one reporter: "Island Records was struck by the album potential of the band, that it wasn't going to be a singles-oriented campaign."

After working hard to establish themselves in their native Ireland, the four ex-Mount Temple students at last had the opportunity to prove to the rest of the world that U2 was a force with which to be reckoned.

CHAPTER III

Shortly after U2 signed the deal with Island Records, studio time was booked at Windmill Lane in Dublin, where the band was to record its first single for the label. Martin Hannett (a.k.a. "Martin Zero") was brought in as the producer and, at the time, he was garnering a good deal of acclaim for his work with bands like Joy Division, the Teardrop Explodes and Orchestral Manoeuvres In The Dark. A former bass player turned booking agent, Hannett had gotten into production, with one of his early projects being the Buzzcocks' superb *Spiral Scratch* Ep. He then became noted for his work with a lot of bands in the Manchester area and was referred to in the *1981 Rock Yearbook* as "undoubtedly the most celebrated British record producer outside London."

U2 had apparently been keen to work with Martin Hannett after they heard his production of Joy Division's UNKNOWN PLEASURES album. Although he generally preferred to work at Strawberry Studios in Manchester, Hannett was persuaded to come over to Dublin.

U2 spent the Easter weekend of 1980 at Windmill Lane Studios, and a month later the debut Island release, *11 O'Clock Tick Tock* (b/w *Touch*), emerged. Although the single earned positive reviews, it failed to register any significant chart impact.

Not to be deterred, the group embarked on its second visit to Britain for another series of London gigs. U2 played gigs at pub/club venues like the Hammersmith Clarendon, the Nashville Rooms and

REDLINE
THE
BRAINS

even the notorious Marquee Club. Although it was still early days, the band was building up a strong following and was garnering a good deal of attention in the press.

By now, Bono was beginning to establish himself as a powerful front-man, and there can be no doubt that his stage presence had been helped by his mime studies with a Dublin drama tutor named Mannix Flynn. The Edge later told American journalist Chris Connelly: "I think Bono did something which not many others did and that was confront a crowd ... he went out there and *assumed* this importance and this character and eyed the audience and was totally impressive."

The members of U2 had also come a long way as a band, and by the time they started preparing for their debut album they had over 40 songs from which they could make their final selection. Although they had wanted to work with Martin Hannett on their first single, they decided to enlist Steve Lillywhite to produce the album.

Lillywhite had started his career as a tape operator at London's Phonogram studios. He then engineered and coproduced records before he moved to Island studios, where he worked until 1979. At this juncture, he became a freelance producer. His early production work included a collaboration with Brian Eno on an Ultravox Lp, after which he handled XTC, Penetration and Siouxsie and the Banshees. When he hooked up with U2 in the summer of 1980, he was riding high on the success of his work on Peter Gabriel's third Lp, which actually topped the U.K. charts in June '80.

Once again, U2 decided to record at Dublin's Windmill Lane Studios. However, when Steve Lillywhite arrived on the scene, he was surprised at the minimal amount of equipment that the band was using. In a 1982 interview with Chas De Whalley (who had left CBS and gone back to music journalism) the Edge recalled: "When we went into the studio to record our first album with Steve Lillywhite, he was as-

tounded at how little gear U2 had as a band. One guitar, one bass, a drumkit and a couple of amps was about the extent of it. We've come on a little since then, of course, but we still believe in keeping things relatively simple."

Despite the fact that U2 had very little equipment, the Edge had invested in an Electroharmonix Memory Man Chorus Echo unit for his guitar, the sound of which was to earn him tremendous notoriety. "We'd been playing our original set of pretty aggressive songs for about a year," says the guitarist. "And I was growing tired of the same old sounds."

The Edge wanted to add more color, not only to his playing, but also to the band's overall sound. Since money was still hard to come by, he knew that whatever effect he bought, it would probably be the only one he could afford for some time. As soon he started using the "Memory Man" during rehearsals, he claims: "The sheer variety of sounds I could get from it seemed to

spark not just me but the rest of the band , too."

The guitarist maintains that for the next month U2 went through a creatively intense period, during which the echo unit inspired them to write two songs a day. He reveals that the song *I Will Follow* fell together in less than 15 minutes! The "Memory Man" prompted the band to work in a way that they had never done before,and the Edge is adamant that the first Lp would have been completely different had he not invested in the gadget.

Following the August of the Steve Lillywhite-produced single, *A Day Without Me* (b/w *Things To Make And Do*), U2's debut album emerged in October. Titled BOY, it featured re-recordings of *Out Of Control*, *Twilight* and *Stories For Boys*, and was an extremely impressive package. It was met with a tremendous amount of enthusiasm from the British music press. Here follows a sampling of some of the reviews.

"A record to place a bit of faith in: a record to lean on and learn from. Next to Echo & The Bunnymen's CROCODILES, it's one of the year's most significant releases a restrained masterpiece." (*Record Mirror*)

"... an overall feeling of loving care and energy intertwined with simplistic and direct hooks and chords." (*Sounds*)

"Like all great rock, you feel you *must* have heard these songs somewhere else—and yet they're unlike any others that you can think of." (*Melody Maker*)

In America, Rolling Stone magazine referred to U2 as "talented, charming and potentially exceptional." However, the reviewer questioned whether the band was actually the "Next Big Thing."

U2 also garnered a lot of media attention for the front cover photograph, which depicted a young boy naked from the waist up. The band and photographer Hugh McGuiness were accused of promoting child pornography. Fortunately, the uproar died down quickly. Bono told reporters that he considered the concept of using a child on the cover to be important because he believed that it connected with the fact that BOY was very much an introduction to the band.

The singer described the Lp as "a summing up of what we are doing, where we come from and where we are going." He also stressed his feelings that BOY was a very unique album, since it was unlike any other record that was coming out of Britain at the time.

Sadly, BOY failed to sell in vast quantities, a fact that wasn't helped by the complete lack of radio airplay given to the songs. Be that as it may, the press support and Island's strong advertising campaign enabled people to become aware of U2. Remember, this was still only the beginning.

CHAPTER IV

oinciding with the release of BOY, U2 embarked on its first major U.K. tour. The band appeared as special guests with Echo & The Bunnymen at London's Lyceum Ballroom and also performed a residency at the Marquee Club. In between the British concerts, the four Irish rockers traveled to Europe for the first time, where they played in Belgium and Holland.

Meanwhile, interest had begun to mount in America, where U2 had attracted the attention of Frank Barsalona at the well-respected Premier Talent booking agency. Barsalona, who handled both Bruce Springsteen and the Who, had allegedly picked up on the band before BOY had even been released. Bono enthusiastically told one Irish music critic that U2 was going to conquer America "like no other British band has broken it in a long time."

Before the end of 1980, a brief East Coast tour had been arranged. The first date was at New York's Mudd Club and Bono subsequently told one British reporter that when the people from the booking agency talked to the band after the show, they said that it was going to be very interesting to see the band perform at New York's giant Madison Square Garden in the future. At this stage, however, massive arena-size gigs held little interest for the band, since they equated them with a total lack of intimacy. Little did they know that in less than five years they would have little difficulty in "getting their message" across to 20,000 fans at the Garden!

After taking a short break over the Christmas holidays, U2 went back on the road at the beginning of 1981. In February, the band headlined the Lyceum in London, with the Thompson Twins appearing as the opening act. The concert was a complete sellout and hundreds of fans were turned away at the door after all the tickets had been sold.

By the spring of '81, U2 had returned to America for a three-month tour. Most of the gigs were club dates, but Warner Brothers (Island Records' U.S. distributors) gave the band "priority treatment." Consequently, while many British bands tend to find the going to be extremely tough on their first American outings, and subsequently develop a sour taste about touring the country, U2 encountered few problems during their trek.

Traveling through the country on a proper tour bus, the group played a string of Mid-West shows in cities like Chicago, Cincinnati and Detroit. U2's debut West Coast appearance was at the Country Club in Los Angeles, where they elicited an incredibly strong reaction from the audience. The band played a 50-minute set during the tour, with most of the material coming from the BOY album, The Lp charted on *Billboard's* Top 100 and *I Will Follow* became extremely popular on college radio stations.

By the time the U.S. dates were over, U2 had been out on the road for six months. Basically, the intention had been to go out and let as many people as possible see what the band was about. The task had most definitely been accomplished.

After the last American show, the group went off to the Bahamas, accompanied by producer Steve Lillywhite, who had been with them during the final leg of the tour discussing ideas for the second album. While vacationing in the Bahamas, U2 spent some time at Compass Point Studios in Nassau, recording a new single, titled *Fire*, which was released in July '81.

By August, U2 had returned to Ireland and, during that month, they put on an incredible show opening for Thin Lizzy at Slane Castle. The band was certainly well on its way to attaining superstar status in its home country, a fact reflected in the results of the *Hot Press* magazine readers' poll. Aside from being ranked "Best Band," BOY was voted "Best Album" and Bono won the "Best Singer" category.

At the Slane Castle concert, U2 aired a number of songs from the upcoming second Lp, which was subsequently recorded at Windmill Lane Studios. The band members had decided to work in Dublin again because they liked the studios and found the environment to be both comfortable and relaxing.

The original title of U2's second album was reportedly SCARLET, but during the recording the band had decided to call the Lp OCTOBER. The album is said to have been made under a lot of pressure, with the material being written and re-corded very quickly. Bono's lyric book had apparently been stolen just before the sessions started, and consequently he was forced to come up with new ideas while he was at the microphone. This must have been quite expensive when one considers the cost of hiring a recording studio.

When OCTOBER was finally released, it proved to be vastly different from its predecessor. Essentially, BOY had been an amalgam of five years worth of material and, for this

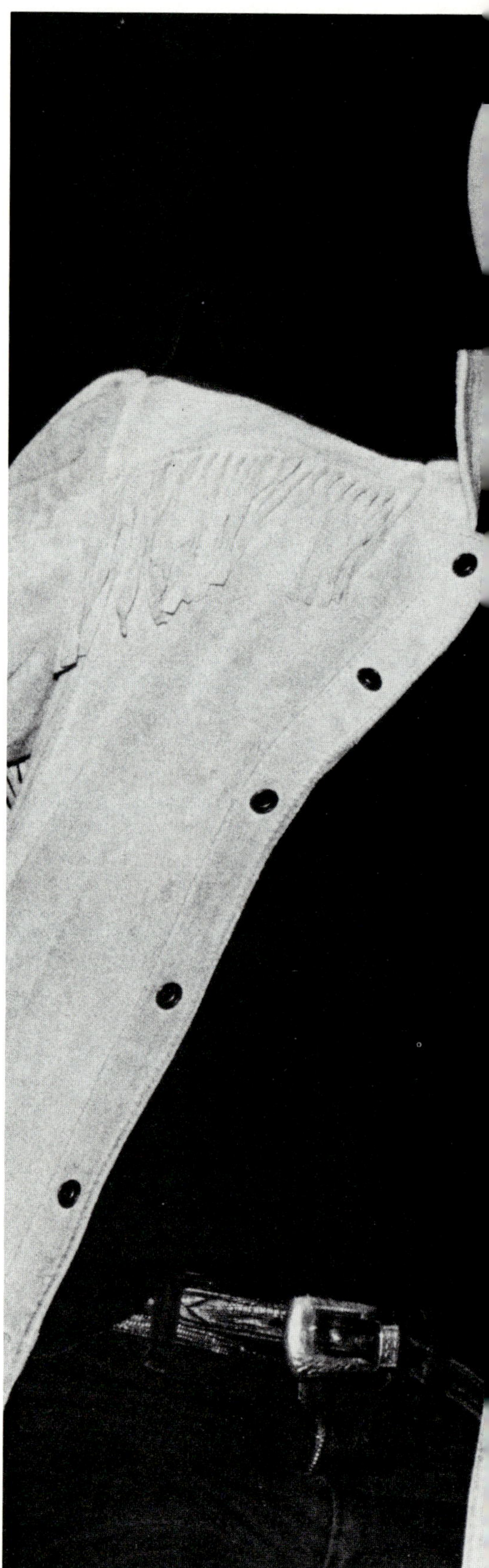

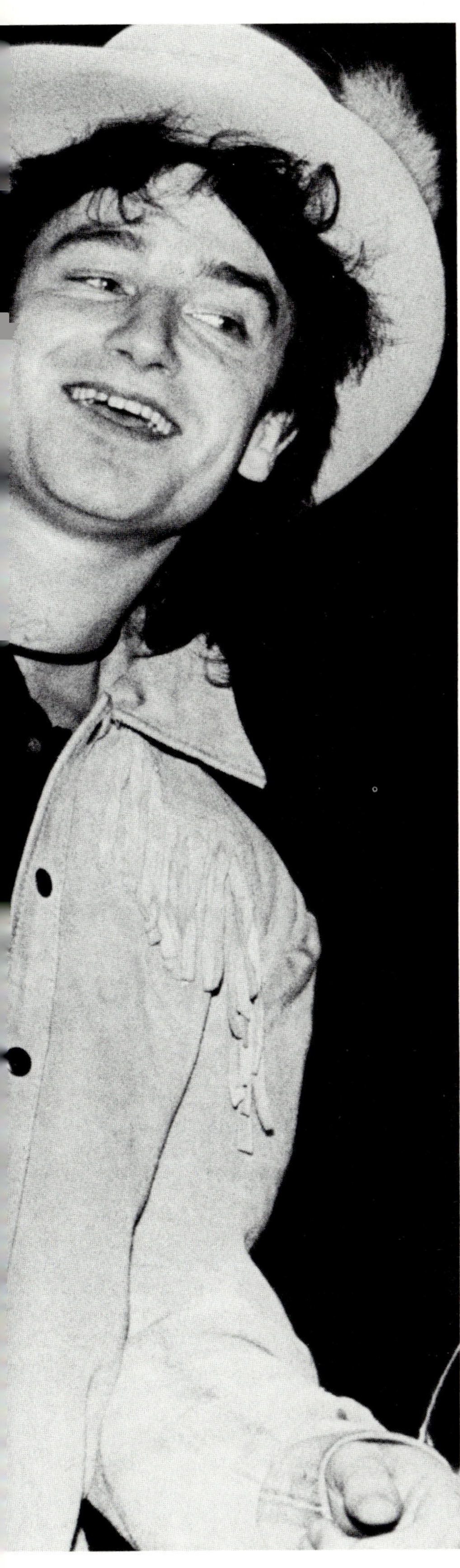

reason, the record had contained a tremendous amount of raw energy. OCTOBER, on the other hand, offered more substance and it definitely displayed the band's maturity.

Kicking off with the anthemic, almost hymn-like *Gloria*, the album featured songs like *Rejoice* and the brilliant *I Threw A Brick*. Many described it as a "Christian Lp" and there can be no question that the members of U2 were very open about displaying their faith. However, it would be grossly unfair to accuse them of preaching heavily or carrying on any kind of crusade.

The Edge told one British writer that U2 had attempted to record something a little less hectic and a little more thoughtful. He maintained that the Lp showed that U2 was progressing and broadening its base, rather than adhering to one particular style. "OCTOBER could so easily have been BOY PART II," he assessed. "But instead it shows us growing up and out. And to my mind that's the way every band should go."

The reaction to OCTOBER was mixed; there were those who liked BOY but were unable to come to terms with the second Lp. However, there were also those who picked up on the band *because* of OCTOBER. The album climbed to the number 11 spot on the British charts and it eventually sold over 250,000 copies, thus earning the group its first silver disc.

In November 1981, the U2 members journeyed back to America for their third U.S. trek in the past year. The audiences were getting bigger all the time and, rather than just performing in major cities, the band played everywhere and anywhere in order to achieve maximum exposure.

By the end of 1981, the U2 members had returned home to Ireland, where they subsequently performed their first concerts in the home country for over a year. After playing gigs in Galway and Cork, they headlined the Main Hall at Dublin's RDS venue. With over 5,000 fans in attendance, it was a triumphant homecoming and proved U2's ability to handle large audiences.

Before long, though, it was back to the United States for another six-week tour. OCTOBER was reasonably well received by the American record-buying public, but the fact that it was hard to get radio airplay had a dampening effect on sales. During the U.S. dates, Larry Mullen Jr., who rarely gives interviews, told writer Abby Rubman: "It would have been great if the radio had picked up on BOY, but that's not the way it happened. It's happening slowly. I believe the radio is going to change and things will work out eventually."

Prior to setting off on the American tour, U2 had recorded a new single at Windmill Lane, titled *A Celebration* (b/w *Trash Trampoline And The Party Girls*) which was released in March 1982.

There had been plans for the band to play in Australia, India, Japan and the Far East after they had completed the American gigs, but in the end the four musicians decided that they wanted to spend more time at home. One can also be sure that they were worried that an intense touring schedule might interfere with the creative preparation for their next album. Besides, they had built up a sizeable following and were certainly in a position to afford themselves a break from the hectic pace of constant road life.

During the summer, they limited their live activity to a few European outdoor concerts. At the Werchter Festival in Belgium, they were featured on a bill that also included Peter Gabriel, Simple Minds and the Eurythmics. The only opportunity for British fans to catch the band was at an appearance with the Police, which was held in Gateshead, England. Proving that they had not forgotten their roots, the Dublin boys also performed in their hometown at the fifth *Hot Press* birthday party. Once again, the band had fared well in the magazine's annual readers' poll.

By August, U2 was back at Windmill Lane Studios, recording the third Lp. There had been rumors that the band might be hooking up with U.S. producer Sandy Pearlman, previously known for his work with Blue Oyster Cult and the Dictators. U2 had apparently been impressed by Pearlman's production of the 1978 Clash Lp, GIVE 'EM ENOUGH ROPE. But, although the Irish group reportedly cut one track with the American producer, things didn't work out and it soon became clear that, once again, Steve Lillywhite would be involved.

Meanwhile, Lillywhite had never before collaborated with an act on more than two consecutive albums. He believed that the working relationship was bound to become stale. However, he decided to take on U2 for the third time, perhaps because he knew that this was *the* crucial album for the band. Island Records, who had always viewed U2's music as a "constantly evolving process," had often said that the group might well make its mark with the third Lp.

The recording sessions ran through November. December saw the band embarking on a brief series of British, European and Irish live dates.

The WAR album finally emerged in February 1983 and it was unquestionably the band's finest opus thus far. Both musically and lyrically, it was a very harsh sounding record, and the Edge told reporters that the group had aimed to be a little more dangerous in order to dispel the "cosy image that people had of U2."

The album kicked off in dramatic fashion with the song, *Sunday Bloody Sunday*, which dealt with the tragic days in Irish history that had occurred during the ongoing civil war. In the past, U2 had stayed clear of writing about the troubles in Northern Ireland. However, the band members claimed that it was after going to America that they had really begun to consider approaching the topic. They felt that *Sunday Bloody Sunday* was an attempt to confront the subject, instead of "sweeping it under the carpet."

The lyrics were intended to draw attention to the tragedy of families that were being destroyed by the constant fighting. U2 was taking no sides, because there were no sides to be taken. Bono confessed to one interviewer that he would like to see a united Ireland because, "after all, it is an island." Asked whether he believes in a cause enough to die for it, his response was that he believes in a cause enough to *live* for it. Furthermore, the singer has continually stressed that *"Sunday Bloody Sunday* is *not* a rebel song."

WAR also boasted outstanding tunes such as the New York funk-influenced *Two Hearts Beat As One* and the driving *New Year's Day*, which dealt with the Soviet domination of Poland. Bono's vocal work had developed considerably, and it seems that Steve Lillywhite had basically pushed him to the max. The singer's wife Alison, whom he had married in 1982, is also said to have motivated him with his lyric writing when he lost inspiration.

The media's reaction to WAR was mixed. Reviewing the album in *The Record*, Christopher Hill assessed: "Though WAR is U2's most controlled and concise set of songs

yet, they still give the same impression of people wrestling desperately, passionately, with something we can't see or feel." The writer went on to add that, "the Lp falls short just where its ambitions are highest."

In another review, the highly respected Kurt Loder declared: "WAR succeeds impressively on the strength of its tempestuous sound, its haunting harmonies and its heartbroken litany of humankind's unceasing inhumanity." While Loder praised songs like *Sunday Bloody Sunday* and *New Year's Day*, he seemed to have certain reservations about some of the Lp's lyrical content. He was quick to point out Bono's line on *Two Hearts Beat As One* about, "not knowing how to say what's got to be said." After a while, though, Loder confessed that such criticism was basically a case of "quibbling."

In actual fact, it didn't really matter what the critics had to say because the general record-buying public around the world welcomed WAR with open arms. The Lp entered the British charts at number one, knocking Michael Jackson's THRILLER album off the top spot. In America, due to strong radio support, over 200,000 copies of WAR were shipped in the first 10 days of its release. The album went on to sell in excess of one million copies and became U2's first U.S. platinum record.

Coinciding with WAR's emergence, the band set off on a marathon global tour, which commenced with 28 dates in Britain. While *Sunday Bloody Sunday* was issued in many countries as the first single from the album, the song was considered too strong for the U.K. and it would have probably received very little airplay from the BBC (British Broadcasting Company), which controls the major radio stations. Consequently, British listeners were presented with *New Year's Day*, the B-side of which featured a previously unreleased studio song called *Treasure (Whatever Happened To Pete The Chop?)*. Pete The Chop was supposedly a friend of the band during

the early days in Dublin, who had once asked Bono to write a song about him.

During the British tour, *Two Hearts Beat As One* was released as the second single from WAR. As an added bonus, the package contained remixes of the A-side and of *New Year's Day.* Island Records' president, Chris Blackwell, had taken the master tapes of the two songs to New York, where the re-mix specialist, Francas Kervorkian, had come up with dance-oriented mixes of the tunes. In America, these helped U2 to gain airplay on dance radio stations, as well as in the clubs.

The band began a two-month U.S. trek in the middle of April and most of the shows were sold out. During the second week of May, while U2 was playing on the East Coast, Bono contracted problems with his throat, which forced him to remain silent during the daytime so that he would be able to sing at night. Fortunately, it wasn't long before he was at his peak again.

At the end of May, U2 performed in front of over 300,000 people at the second US Festival, which was held in San Bernadino, California. Bono had established himself as an incredibly charismatic frontman and during the US Festival show, he climbed to the top of the giant stage and put up a flag. He later stated that he regarded it as a symbol, "a broadstroke to that mass of people."

During the WAR tour, Bono had started holding a white flag during *Sunday Bloody Sunday.* He told the press that he wanted to get away from Ireland's national green, white and orange flag, Britain's union jack or America's stars and stripes. He apparently wished that all of the colors could be drained from flags.

Aside from the US Festival, U2 also played a huge outdoor show at the Red Rocks Auditorium in Denver, Colorado. Bonfires were burning around the natural amphitheatre-style venue while the band was on-

stage, and it proved to be an extremely spectacular concert. British fans were able to catch the action on Channel 4's *Midsummer Night's Tube* TV show. An edited version of the set was subsequently released worldwide in a home video format called LIVE AT RED ROCKS UNDER A BLOOD RED SKY. Even on video, it was incredible to watch the concert, although the Edge has said that the fact that it was pouring with rain aided the film's visual appeal, since the dampness of the air made everything look particularly atmospheric.

Bruce Springsteen attended the band's Philadelphia concert and Bono actually dedicated one of the encores to "Steel Mill"— the name of one of Springsteen's early bands. After the show, "The Boss" joined the four members of U2 for dinner. Bono enjoyed a lengthy conversation with Springsteen, during which he apparently told him how much he had enjoyed his NEBRASKA album because of the fragile quality of the music.

Upon completion of their 1983 North American tour, the Irish rockers returned home, where they headlined the Phoenix Park Festival in Dublin on Sunday, August 14. The bill also featured Steel Pulse, Big Country, the Eurythmics and Simple Minds, and over 20,000 fans turned up to witness the event. U2's performance was quite emotional, with Bono reportedly bringing his father onstage for a "swift jig." It was also the Edge's birthday and the massive crowd joined in to sing a rousing rendition of *Happy Birthday*. The set had comprised songs from all of the band's studio albums, although only three songs were aired from OCTOBER. For their first encore, the group gave the fans a sneak preview of a new tune titled *Party Girl*. However, when the concert was over, Bono allegedly stated that the day had represented the final chapter in the first part of the U2 story.

U2
4
THE
PEOPLE

CHAPTER V

Towards the end of 1983, U2 released the mini-Lp, UNDER A BLOOD RED SKY, which featured two tracks from the Red Rocks show in Denver, together with live recordings from concerts in Boston and Germany. Island Records was obviously delighted to be able to market more U2 product and the Lp was eventually certified gold for sales of over 500,000 copies in the United States. There can be no doubt that the record also helped to lower the volume of illegal bootleg recordings of the band's live performances.

UNDER A BLOOD RED SKY was produced by Jimmy Iovine, who is famous for his work with the likes of Tom Petty and Dire Straits. After becoming a keen U2 fan, Iovine is said to have offered to work on the live record for "next to nothing." However, despite its commercial success, the band did not consider Jimmy Iovine the right man to produce the next studio Lp.

After making the WAR album, both the group and Steve Lillywhite had mutually agreed not to work on another record together—at least for the time being. As the Edge informed writer Bruce Nixon: "Our relationship with Steve is still fantastic and I'd work with him tomorrow. But we thought that the tension of working with someone new might be inspiring, and it was. With Steve, that tension was no longer there."

While it was rumored that U2 might be employing Conny Plank to work on the new album, it was soon announced that Brian Eno would be at the production helm.

A member of Roxy Music during the early 70s, Eno had subsequently recorded a series of abstract electronic albums such as MUSIC FOR AIRPORTS and MUSIC FOR FILMS. As a producer, he had made his mark working with David Bowie on the LOW/HEROES/LODGER trilogy and with the Talking Heads on three albums—MORE SONGS ABOUT BUILDINGS AND FOOD, FEAR OF MUSIC and REMAIN IN LIGHT.

U2 initially contacted Brian Eno during the summer of '83, but he is said to have turned them down. Not to be deterred, the Irish band kept nagging him until he agreed to sit down and talk. Eno was apparently intrigued with Bono when he finally met the singer, but he warned the group that, if he worked on the record, it would probably end up sounding like nothing they had ever done before. And that is exactly what U2 wanted. Although it would have been a guaranteed success, the band had absolutely no intention of making WAR: PART TWO.

U2's contract with Island Records had recently been renegotiated and the company president, Chris Blackwell, was reportedly concerned when he found out that the group intended to hire Brian Eno. When Blackwell came to Dublin to see the four musicians, they told him that if he had come with a view to protecting his investment then he should leave. On the other hand, they said that if he had come as a fan, then he was more than welcome to stay. In the end, the record executive spent enough time with them to understand why they had chosen Brian Eno.

Since U2 had recorded the first three studio albums at Windmill Lane in Dublin, it was felt that a change of environment might have a beneficial effect on the new material. After searching for a place to record during the spring of 1984, the band decided to set up base at the stately home of Slane Castle in County Meath, a short distance from Dublin. A mobile recording studio was brought into the drawing room and the basic instrumental playing was done in the library, where the acoustics were particularly strong since they had been designed to accomodate chamber music recitals.

U2 spent two weeks with Brian Eno, just throwing ideas around before the proper recording sessions commenced. The Edge has said that the producer was particularly useful in helping them to simplify the overall structure of the songs. Accompanying Eno was a Canadian named Daniel Lanois, who served as his engineer and collaborator. It proved to be a good team and the Edge claims that Lenois' knowledge of notation and manuscript music enabled him to communicate with the band in a way that Steve Lillywhite had never done.

The recording of the album lasted a good deal longer than had originally been anticipated and one senses that the band members allowed themselves the luxury of experimenting with different sounds and ideas. Apparently, over 25 pieces of music were recorded and the Edge has stated that the group had some very successful improvisations, which were unlike anything that had been done before. A lot of these were considered inappropriate for the album, but the guitarist claimed that it was possible that they would be released at some point in the future.

Bono has also said that the Lp was delayed because of the lyric writing. Towards the end of the project, things became hectic, as the band had to shoot the cover shots for the album with photographer Anton Corbijn, film a video for the first single and then conduct a series of press interviews.

While the basic recording was done at Slane Castle, U2 returned to Windmill Lane for the final mixing sessions. By this stage, things were moving ahead swiftly, since Brian Eno's time was limited due to other commitments. Also, U2 was set to embark on a tour of Australia.

In September, the band issued the first single from the new Lp. Titled *Pride (In The Name Of Love)*, the lyrics were inspired by the life of the late Martin Luther King. The original musical ideas for the song had stemmed from a soundcheck in Hawaii and Bono had apparently started off writing the words about Ronald Reagan. He eventually decided that King was better subject matter, although it must be pointed out that the singer was guilty of an historical inaccuracy, stating that the man had been assassinated in the morning and not early evening, as had been the case. Be that as it may, *Pride* was an excellent song and it registered significant chart impact around the world.

A few weeks after the single had come out, U2 released its fourth studio album, THE UNFORGETTABLE FIRE. The band had taken the title for the Lp from a series of drawings that had been done by the survivors of the Hiroshima and Nagasaki bombings. *The Unforgettable Fire Exhibition* had opened at the Chicago Peace Museum in the fall of 1982 and U2 had actually donated the WAR backdrop and stage set to the museum.

The UNFORGETTABLE FIRE

turned out to be the band's finest album to date and it differed a great deal from WAR. Adam Clayton believed that U2's fourth studio release echoed the innocence of BOY, but he felt that it also contained the powerful atmospherics of OCTOBER. Aside from *Pride (In The Name Of Love)*, the Lp boasted a wealth of top quality material.

The title song featured a superb string arrangement and was incredibly well textured. On *Promenade*, Bono proved that both his singing and his lyric writing had matured tremendously. The strangest tune on the record was *Elvis Presley & America*, which saw Bono airing his vocal chords over a backing track that Brian Eno had slowed down. It was an extremely raw piece and the singer was reportedly dubious about releasing it until Eno convinced him otherwise.

On the guitar front, the Edge had also changed his approach and come up with a softer, richer sound. He was determined not to duplicate his playing on WAR because he felt that it had become a little too familiar and, in one technical interview, he confessed that it worried him when people started talking about a "classic Edge sound."

By the time THE UNFORGETTABLE FIRE emerged, U2 was back on the road for the start of yet another protracted touring stint. The band members had maintained a low profile throughout much of 1984 and their return to concert stages was eagerly awaited by fans around the world. Bono had actually made a one-off public appearance during the summer, when he joined Bob Dylan onstage in Dublin. It wasn't a particularly memorable event in rock'n'roll history, though, since the U2 singer basically had to "bluff" his way through a couple of Dylan's songs, due to the fact that he didn't know the lyrics! Word has it that Bono had received the invitation to go onstage courtesy of Bob Dylan's son, who happens to be a big U2 fan.

U2's 1984-85 touring schedule saw the band playing concerts in

Australia, New Zealand, Germany, Italy, France, Belgium, Switzerland, Holland, Britain and, of course, North America.

There were a few pre-Christmas '84 shows in the U.S., but the group's fullscale assault on North American concert halls began at the end of February, 1985, at the Dallas Reunion Arena. After playing a number of gigs in Texas, U2 traveled to the West Coast and then on to Honolulu, Hawaii. After a few days off in the Hawaiian islands, the band continued its tour with dates in Denver, Minneapolis, Chicago, Detroit and Cleveland. At the end of March, U2 performed three Canadian concerts and then on April 1 the band arrived in New York City to play Madison Square Garden.

In an interview with Britain's *New Musical Express*, Bono talked about the arena-sized venues that U2 was appearing at in the U.S. and declared: "That was everything we were against, and we were against playing these aircraft hangers right up to the time I went to see Bruce Springsteen at Wembley Arena (a 10,000-seat venue in London). Now, I enjoy these places—instead of a backdrop of stained glass windows, we've got people ... that's it, *people*! And we *are* making big music! When we start *Pride*, that *floats* over the audience and to confine it is a living lie."

U2's performance at Madison Square Garden was absolutely incredible. 20,000 New York fans turned up to witness the event and very few could have left the venue disappointed.

After starting the show with *11 O'Clock Tick Tock*, U2 launched into a powerful version of *I Will Follow*. The rest of the set featured an excellent selection of material from all four of the band's studio releases. During the first of several encores, Bono asked if anyone in the crowd could play guitar. A young lad in the audience was quick to jump onstage, where he was given an acoustic guitar by the singer, who taught him to play the chords to Bob Dylan's *Knockin' On Heaven's Door*. The

fact that the fan couldn't play a note didn't really matter! As always, Bono and the band were simply trying to maintain a level of intimacy with their audiences. The New York City concert was finally brought to a close with rousing renditions of *Gloria* and *40*.

U2 spent the rest of April performing on the East Coast. At the end of the month, when the band played in Atlanta, the four members were invited to the Martin Luther King Center. It was a memorable experience, one that they won't easily forget. A few days later, the North American tour ended in Florida.

U2's British fans were able to catch the band in action at a huge outdoor festival called "The Longest Day," which was held at the Milton Keynes Bowl on Saturday, June 22. Like most festivals that take place in England, the show was marred by a torrential downpour of rain. The ground soon turned to mud and thousands of fans were soaked as they watched a bill that featured Spear Of Destiny, Billy Bragg, the Ramones, R.E.M. and, finally, U2. A review in one of the British music papers stated: "There was no doubt at all that U2 brought renewed energy to a cold, bedraggled and frustrated audience."

A week later, the Irish band played to over 55,000 fans at Croke Park in Dublin and, happily, the hometown fans were able to enjoy the show in better weather than the Milton Keynes audience had to contend with. Not surprisingly, the Dublin concert was an unqualified success from start to finish.

U2 appeared at a festival in Belgium at the beginning of July, on a bill that also included Paul Young, Depeche Mode, the Style Council, R.E.M. and the Ramones. On July 13, the Irish rockers took part in the London *Live Aid* concert and their performance was unquestionably one of the highlights of the day's incredible feast of music. The band had been eager to play at Wembley, particularly since Bono and Adam Clayton had both been fea-

tured on the original Band Aid single, *Do They Know It's Christmas?/ Feed The World*.

Aside from a surprise appearance in front of 6,000 fans at a free concert in Cork, Ireland, in September, there was to be very little activity on the U2 front during the rest of '85. Island Records issued an Ep, titled WIDE AWAKE IN AMERICA, which included a live version of *Bad*, together with three other songs—*A Sort Of Homecoming* (produced by Tony Visconti), *Three Sun Rises* and *Love Comes Tumbling*. However, most U2 fans were eagerly awaiting the group's next studio album, which is scheduled to emerge sometime in 1986.

And what does the future hold for the Irish supergroup? Bono maintains that the band still has ambitions and that these are definitely not simply to make more money. He is adamant that if U2's objective had been to attain fame and fortune, the band would have already reached the end of the road. As he recently told *Rolling Stone*: "We have this light in the distance. I don't know what it is, a musical goal or what. But we're certain that we're going toward it. We're always arguing with each other and pushing people out of the way so we can get there. But it's for the *music*, it's not for the other things."

U2 ... 4 the people.

BY CHERRY LANE BOOKS

Now that you've enjoyed this edition of the ROCK READ series, here's your opportunity to check out all the other fine books in our catalogue. If you want the best biographies, fully illustrated of course, of your favorite music stars, then simply send us your name and address and we'll put you on our mailing list. With many official authorized biographies, you know you're getting the goods. Whether your taste in music is easy listening, new wave, country or heavy metal, if you want the best in rock reading—we've got it! Write to ROCK READ, Dept. #8647, P.O. Box 341, Rye, NY 10580.